THE COLDEST OF THE COLD

The COLDEST of the Cold

Walter the Educator

Silent King Books

SILENT KING BOOKS

SKB

Copyright © 2024 by Walter the Educator

All rights reserved. No part of this book may be reproduced in any manner whatsoever without written permission except in the case of brief quotations embodied in critical articles and reviews.

First Printing, 2024

Disclaimer
This book is a literary work; poems are not about specific persons, locations, situations, and/or circumstances unless mentioned in a historical context. This book is for entertainment and informational purposes only. The author and publisher offer this information without warranties expressed or implied. No matter the grounds, neither the author nor the publisher will be accountable for any losses, injuries, or other damages caused by the reader's use of this book. The use of this book acknowledges an understanding and acceptance of this disclaimer.

The Coldest of the Cold is a basketball story about a player who overcame a life obstacle to become great. This little collectible short story is by Walter the Educator. Collect more books at WaltertheEducator.com.

THE COLDEST OF THE COLD

In the heart of rural Indiana, a basketball prodigy named Jordan Halsey emerged, destined to etch his name into the annals of sports history. From a young age, it was clear that Jordan possessed a transcendent talent. He danced with the basketball, his movements so fluid and graceful that spectators swore he was born with the game in his blood.

The COLDEST of the Cold

Jordan's journey began at Marston High, where he led his team to four consecutive state championships. His high school career was a spectacle of soaring dunks, pinpoint passes, and defensive prowess that left opponents in awe.

The COLDEST of the Cold

In his junior year at Marston High, Jordan Halsey played a game that would forever be etched into the memories of those who witnessed it. It was the state championship game against their arch-rival, Pinecrest High. The anticipation was palpable, the atmosphere electric, and the stakes higher than ever. Both teams had been undefeated all season, and this game would determine the true champion.

The COLDEST of the Cold

From the moment the ball was tipped, it was clear that this was no ordinary game. Pinecrest came out strong, their star player, Eric Marshall, showcasing his formidable skills. The first quarter saw Pinecrest take an early lead, but Jordan was undeterred. He was known for his calm under pressure and his ability to elevate his game when it mattered most.

The COLDEST of the Cold

As the second quarter began, Jordan took control. He executed a series of plays that left the crowd in awe. First, he intercepted a pass at midcourt and sprinted towards the basket, finishing with a thunderous dunk that ignited the Marston fans. His defense was impeccable, shutting down Marshall with relentless pressure and lightning-quick reflexes.

The COLDEST of the Cold

With each possession, Jordan displayed a masterful blend of finesse and power. He hit a fadeaway jumper from the baseline, then followed it up with a three-pointer from well beyond the arc, his form perfect, his confidence unshakeable. Pinecrest defenders tried double-teaming him, but Jordan's court vision allowed him to make precise passes to open teammates, resulting in easy baskets.

The COLDEST of the Cold

By halftime, Marston had closed the gap, trailing by only a few points. In the locker room, Jordan's leadership shone through as he rallied his teammates, his words a potent mix of encouragement and tactical advice. His belief in their ability to win was contagious.

The COLDEST of the Cold

The second half was a showcase of Jordan's unparalleled versatility. He drove to the basket with ferocity, finishing with acrobatic layups that seemed to defy gravity. His mid-range game was unstoppable, each shot a testament to his meticulous preparation and natural talent. On defense, he was a wall, blocking shots and stealing the ball with uncanny precision.

The COLDEST of the Cold

With the game tied in the final minute, the tension was unbearable. Marston had possession, and the ball was in Jordan's hands. As the clock ticked down, he dribbled at the top of the key, his eyes scanning the court.

The COLDEST of the Cold

With ten seconds left, he made his move, driving past his defender with a quick crossover. Two Pinecrest players converged on him, but Jordan anticipated their move. He spun away, rising for a shot just beyond the free-throw line.

The COLDEST of the Cold

Time seemed to stand still as the ball arced towards the basket. The swish of the net was the only sound in the silent gymnasium. Marston was ahead by two. Pinecrest had one last chance, but Jordan intercepted the inbound pass, securing the victory.

The COLDEST of the Cold

The final score was 78-76, and Jordan had scored 45 points, with 10 rebounds, 8 assists, 6 steals, and 4 blocks. It was a performance for the ages, a game that transcended statistics. He had displayed every aspect of the game at an elite level: scoring, passing, defense, and leadership. His poise under pressure and ability to dominate in crucial moments solidified his reputation as the greatest anyone had ever seen.

The COLDEST of the Cold

Years later, people still talked about that night. Coaches used it as a teaching tool, players watched the footage in awe, and fans reminisced about the time they saw Jordan Halsey at his absolute best. That game wasn't just a display of talent; it was a testament to his dedication, his love for the game, and his innate ability to rise to the occasion. It was the game that made Jordan Halsey a legend.

The COLDEST of the Cold

He was a local legend, adored by fans and respected by foes. Every scout in the nation had their eyes on him, and every college coach dreamed of having Jordan on their roster.

Choosing to stay close to home, Jordan accepted a full scholarship to Indiana University, where he instantly became the heart and soul of the Hoosiers. His freshman year, he led the team to an improbable national championship, a feat he repeated for the next two seasons.

The COLDEST of the Cold

Jordan was a magician on the court, conjuring plays out of thin air, making the impossible seem routine. Analysts and fans alike whispered that he was even better than Michael Jordan, a claim that seemed blasphemous until they witnessed his greatness firsthand.

The COLDEST of the Cold

Jordan's senior year was poised to be the crown jewel of his illustrious career. The Hoosiers were favorites to win yet another championship, and Jordan's name was already being mentioned in conversations about the NBA draft.

The COLDEST of the Cold

Scouts drooled over his potential, envisioning a future where he dominated the professional league. It was not a question of if he would be the first overall pick, but rather how quickly he would revolutionize the game.

The COLDEST of the Cold

In the NCAA championship game, with the stadium packed to the rafters and millions watching at home, tragedy struck. In the first half, while executing one of his signature drives to the basket, Jordan's knee buckled.

The COLDEST of the Cold

The crowd fell silent as he crumpled to the floor, clutching his leg in agony. The severity of the injury was immediately apparent; the dream was shattered in an instant.

The Hoosiers fought valiantly without their leader, but the magic was gone. They lost the game, and with it, the fairytale ending everyone had envisioned for Jordan.

The diagnosis was devastating: a torn ACL and significant ligament damage. Surgery and rehabilitation could not restore him to his former glory. The NBA, once a certainty, now became an unreachable horizon.

The COLDEST of the Cold

Despite the heartbreak, Jordan's spirit remained unbroken. He graduated with honors, his academic achievements a testament to his resilience and intellect.

The COLDEST of the Cold

He returned to Indiana University as an assistant coach, where he inspired young players with his wisdom and unwavering passion for the game. The community rallied around him, and his legend grew not just as a player but as a mentor and leader.

The COLDEST of the Cold

Jordan Halsey never graced the professional courts, but his legacy transcended the boundaries of the hardwood. He was a symbol of excellence, humility, and perseverance.

The COLDEST of the Cold

His story was one of what could have been, but also of what was — a glorious journey marked by unparalleled skill, boundless love from fans, and an indomitable spirit that inspired generations.

The COLDEST of the Cold

Jordan Halsey was more than the greatest player who never played professionally; he was the heart and soul of basketball itself.

The COLDEST of the Cold

Years passed, and Jordan Halsey became a fixture in the Indiana community, his presence a comforting reminder of the glory days of Hoosier basketball. His impact extended far beyond the court; he was a beloved figure in the town, known for his kindness, generosity, and dedication to nurturing young talent.

The COLDEST of the Cold

He founded the Halsey Hoops Foundation, aimed at providing underprivileged youth with opportunities to excel both academically and athletically.

The COLDEST of the Cold

Under Jordan's guidance, countless young players discovered their potential. He coached with an emphasis on fundamentals and teamwork, instilling in his protégés the values that had defined his own career: hard work, humility, and a love for the game.

The COLDEST of the Cold

His story served as a powerful lesson in resilience and adaptability, showing that even when life takes an unexpected turn, one's passion and purpose can still shine brightly.

One of the most promising talents to emerge from his program was a young player named Marcus Lane. Marcus had grown up idolizing Jordan, his bedroom walls plastered with posters of the legendary Hoosier. Under Jordan's mentorship, Marcus blossomed into a star, his game a blend of natural talent and learned discipline.

The COLDEST of the Cold

By his senior year in high school, Marcus led his team to the state championships, drawing comparisons to a young Jordan Halsey.

The COLDEST of the Cold

During this time, Jordan's old college coach, now the head coach of a struggling NBA team, reached out to him with an intriguing proposition.

The COLDEST of the Cold

He wanted Jordan to join his staff as an assistant coach, believing that Jordan's unique perspective and basketball IQ could be instrumental in turning the franchise around. It was an opportunity for Jordan to finally be a part of the professional league, albeit in a different capacity.

The COLDEST of the Cold

After much deliberation, Jordan accepted the offer. He moved to the city, bringing with him a renewed sense of purpose. The transition to the professional level was challenging, but Jordan's passion and understanding of the game quickly earned him the respect of the players and coaching staff.

The COLDEST of the Cold

His innovative strategies and motivational speeches began to bear fruit, and the team's performance improved significantly.

The COLDEST of the Cold

Meanwhile, Marcus Lane received a full scholarship to Indiana University, continuing the legacy Jordan had left behind. He wore Jordan's old number, 23, as a tribute to his mentor. Under the watchful eye of Jordan's former assistant coach, now the head coach, Marcus led the Hoosiers to another national championship, rekindling the magic of the Halsey era.

The COLDEST of the Cold

Jordan's contributions to the professional team did not go unnoticed. Within a few years, he was promoted to head coach, a role in which he excelled.

The COLDEST of the Cold

His team, once at the bottom of the league, became a formidable force, reaching the playoffs for the first time in over a decade. Jordan's journey from the small-town prodigy to an NBA coach was a testament to his resilience and enduring love for the game.

The COLDEST of the Cold

In the end, Jordan Halsey's story was not one of unfulfilled potential, but of a different kind of greatness. He had influenced countless lives, both on and off the court, and had shown that true success is measured not by personal accolades, but by the positive impact one has on others.

The COLDEST of the Cold

His legacy lived on through the players he mentored, the fans he inspired, and the community he uplifted. Jordan Halsey had become more than a legend; he was a beacon of hope, proving that even in the face of adversity, one's passion and purpose can illuminate the path to greatness.

The COLDEST of the Cold

ABOUT THE CREATOR

Walter the Educator is one of the pseudonyms for Walter Anderson. Formally educated in Chemistry, Business, and Education, he is an educator, an author, a diverse entrepreneur, and he is the son of a disabled war veteran. "Walter the Educator" shares his time between educating and creating. He holds interests and owns several creative projects that entertain, enlighten, enhance, and educate, hoping to inspire and motivate you.

Follow, find new works, and stay up to date with Walter the Educator™ at WaltertheEducator.com

www.ingramcontent.com/pod-product-compliance
Lightning Source LLC
LaVergne TN
LVHW021240080526
838199LV00088B/5292